# MICHIGAN WOLVERINES

BY

MARGARET WEBER

INSIDE COLLEGE FOOTBALL

MEDIA ENHANCED BOOKS
AV2 BY WEIGL
ADDED VALUE • AUDIO VISUAL

www.av2books.com

AV² provides enriched content that supplements and complements this book. Weigl's AV² books strive to create inspired learning and engage young minds in a total learning experience.

## Your AV² Media Enhanced books come alive with...

**Audio**
Listen to sections of the book read aloud.

**Key Words**
Study vocabulary, and complete a matching word activity.

**Video**
Watch informative video clips.

**Quizzes**
Test your knowledge.

**Embedded Weblinks**
Gain additional information for research.

**Slideshow**
View images and captions, and prepare a presentation.

**Try This!**
Complete activities and hands-on experiments.

**... and much, much more!**

Go to **www.av2books.com,** and enter this book's unique code.

**BOOK CODE**

**AVT42334**

**AV² by Weigl** brings you media enhanced books that support active learning.

Published by AV² by Weigl
350 5th Avenue, 59th Floor
New York, NY 10118
Website: www.av2books.com



Library of Congress Control Number: 2018968208

ISBN 978-1-7911-0096-4 (hardcover)
ISBN 978-1-7911-0097-1 (multi-user eBook)
ISBN 978-1-7911-0098-8 (single-user eBook)

Printed in Guangzhou, China
1 2 3 4 5 6 7 8 9 0 23 22 21 20 19

042019
102318

Project Coordinator: Jared Siemens Designer: Terry Paulhus



The publisher acknowledges Alamy, Getty Images, Newscom, and Wikimedia Commons as its primary image suppliers for this title.

INSIDE COLLEGE FOOTBALL

# Michigan Wolverines

## CONTENTS

# Introduction

The Michigan Wolverines began playing football in the late 1800s. This early beginning has given the Wolverines a long and proud tradition. The University of Michigan is credited with introducing the game to other colleges, such as the University of Notre Dame. The teams' **rivalry** began on November 23, 1887, when the Wolverines played Notre Dame for the first time. It is one of the oldest rivalries in college football.

Today, the Wolverines are known as one of the best college football teams. They hold the record for most all-time wins. This alone is something for fans to root for, but there is much more to Wolverines football. The Wolverines bring energy and enthusiasm to their games, especially those against rivals such as Ohio State University. They meet the Ohio State Buckeyes every year in an end-of-season game that brings thousands of fans to the sidelines. The Wolverines have had four consecutive winning seasons under Coach Jim Harbaugh, and they are hopeful that another championship is in their future.

Wolverines tight end Sean McKeon had a career high of 82 yards for five receptions in a 2017 game against the Purdue University Boilermakers.

Tight end Zach Gentry was named Michigan's Offensive Player of the Week after recording seven receptions in a 2018 game against the University of Maryland Terrapins.

# MICHIGAN

**Stadium** Michigan Stadium

**Division** Big Ten East

**Head Coach** Jim Harbaugh

**Location** Ann Arbor, Michigan

**National Championships** 5

**Nicknames** Wolverines

**3**
Heisman Memorial Trophy Winners

**20**
Head Coaches

**4**
Home Stadiums

**82**
Consensus All-Americans

# History

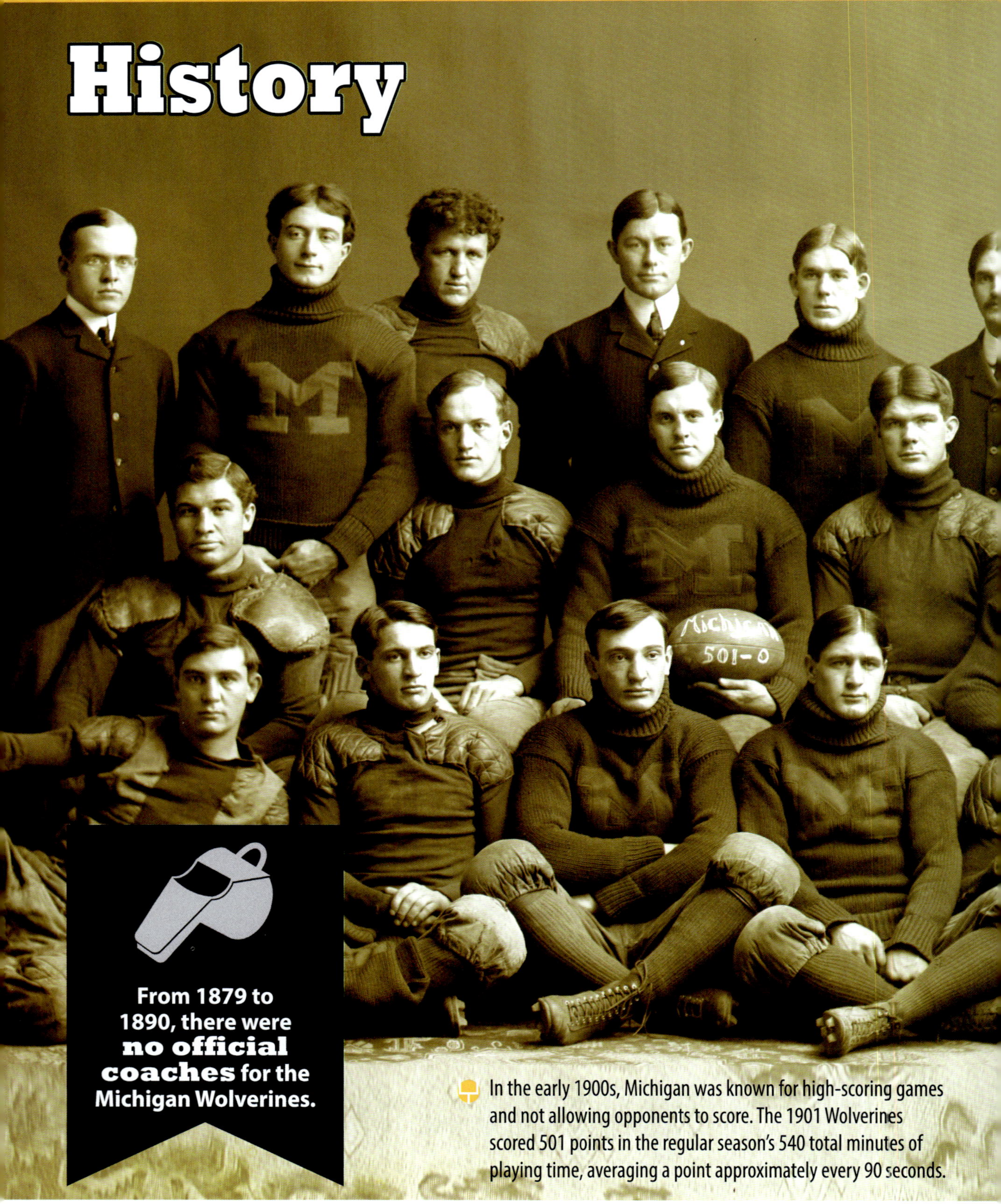


From 1879 to 1890, there were **no official coaches** for the Michigan Wolverines.

In the early 1900s, Michigan was known for high-scoring games and not allowing opponents to score. The 1901 Wolverines scored 501 points in the regular season's 540 total minutes of playing time, averaging a point approximately every 90 seconds.

The first game of football ever played by the Michigan Wolverines was on May 30, 1879. The game was played at White Stocking Park in Chicago, Illinois. Although it looked a bit like rugby, it would eventually become the game that is played today. In 1896, the University of Michigan was part of the **founding** of the Intercollegiate Conference of Faculty Representatives along with six other major universities. This conference would later become the Big Ten Conference.

Under the leadership of Coach Fielding H. Yost, the Wolverines established themselves as a dominant team. They did not lose a single game between 1901 and 1904. This was also the era in which the Wolverines claimed their first National Championships. During the following decades, Michigan continued to excel. In the 1930s and 1940s, the team continued to end seasons with winning records. It also debuted a new form of play that specialized in offensive and defensive teams. This would go on to become standard across all football.

In the modern era of football, Michigan has sought new ways to set player and team records. Its long-time rivalries have set the stage for some of college football's most memorable games, and fans flock in greater numbers each year to cheer for the team.

Music student Louis Elbel wrote the Wolverines' well-known fight song, "The Victors," after a narrow 12–11 Michigan victory over rival University of Chicago in 1898.

# The Stadium

When plans for a new stadium were being developed in 1924, Coach Fielding Yost claimed Michigan would someday need a stadium that seated between 125,000 and 150,000 people.

The Wolverines play in Michigan Stadium. It is one of the most well-known stadiums in all of college sports. Fans and players call it the Big House. This is not an **exaggeration**. Michigan Stadium is the largest sports stadium in the country. The listed capacity of the stadium is 107,601, but it has set records for attendance that surpass that number.

Going into the Big House is a unique experience. It was most recently expanded and **renovated** in 2010. Blue and maize, a particular shade of yellow, are incorporated into the seating, the field, and the hallways. "Michigan" is spelled out in yellow lettering on each end of the field. Two scoreboards were added during the 2010 renovation measuring 4,000 square feet (372 square meters) each. During games, fans cheer and the marching band plays, making the experience loud and exciting.

In addition to hosting football games, Michigan Stadium hosts special events. In 2014, a soccer match between Real Madrid and Manchester United set an attendance record. An amazing 109,318 fans came to the game, the most ever to attend a soccer match in the United States.

It took the university six months to install the new scoreboards at Michigan Stadium during its renovation.

# Where They Play

Welcome to Michigan Stadium. Die-hard fans turn out rain or shine to cheer on their team. For almost a century, crowds have filled the stadium for home football games. A winning team, a top marching band, and many fan traditions make Michigan Stadium one of college football's best.

### BIG TEN WEST

1. **Northwestern University**
   *Evanston, Illinois*
2. **Purdue University**
   *West Lafayette, Indiana*
3. **University of Illinois**
   *Urbana-Champaign, Illinois*
4. **University of Iowa**
   *Iowa City, Iowa*
5. **University of Minnesota**
   *Minneapolis, Minnesota*
6. **University of Nebraska**
   *Lincoln, Nebraska*
7. **University of Wisconsin**
   *Madison, Wisconsin*

**Arena**
Michigan Stadium

**Location**
Ann Arbor, Michigan

**Broke Ground**
1926

**Completed**
1927

**Surface**
Artificial Turf

**Features**
- A 2010 renovation cost $226 million
- All audio in the stadium comes from the press box
- The stadium has hosted night games since 2011

### BIG TEN EAST

1. **Indiana University**
   *Bloomington, Indiana*
2. **Michigan State University**
   *East Lansing, Michigan*
3. **Ohio State University**
   *Columbus, Ohio*
4. **Pennsylvania State University**
   *State College, Pennsylvania*
5. **Rutgers University–New Brunswick**
   *New Brunswick–Piscataway, New Jersey*
6. **University of Maryland**
   *College Park, Maryland*
7. ★ **University of Michigan**
   *Ann Arbor, Michigan*

NORTH DAKOTA
MINNESOTA
WISCONSIN
MICHIGAN
NEW YORK
RHODE ISLAND
CONNECTICUT
NEW JERSEY
SOUTH DAKOTA
PENNSYLVANIA
IOWA
NEBRASKA
ILLINOIS
INDIANA
OHIO
DELAWARE
MARYLAND
WASHINGTON, D.C.
WEST VIRGINIA
VIRGINIA
KANSAS
MISSOURI
KENTUCKY
NORTH CAROLINA
TENNESSEE
SOUTH CAROLINA
OKLAHOMA
ARKANSAS
MISSISSIPPI
ALABAMA
GEORGIA
Atlantic Ocean
TEXAS
LOUISIANA
FLORIDA
Gulf of Mexico
SCALE
0 miles
500 miles
0 kilometers
500 km
LEGEND
Home Stadium
Big Ten West
Big Ten East
United States
Other Countries
Water

# The Uniforms

In **2017**, the Wolverines played in an **all-maize jersey** against the University of Florida. It was the first time they did so since 1928.

The 2011 Wolverines throwback uniform combined elements from different eras of Michigan football. The Wolverines wore the uniform in their first-ever night game at Michigan Stadium.

The Wolverines proudly sport the colors maize and blue. The team's maize color is instantly recognizable to fans all over the country. The traditional uniform of the Wolverines has maize pants and a blue jersey. The helmet fans know and love was introduced in 1938. Coach Herbert "Fritz" Crisler created a winged design. The helmet is blue with maize wings extending back across the sides and top. The Michigan Wolverines' winged helmet design is considered the most well-known in college football.

Like many college football teams, the Wolverines play in alternate jerseys for special events and games. For example, in 2011, Michigan replaced the large numbers on the front with an M for a game against Notre Dame. These distinctive jerseys give the team the chance to show off unique looks.

Coach Jim Harbaugh uses blue and yellow football-shaped helmet stickers to foster competition between players. Players receive stickers for exceptional performances in games.

# Student Athletes

In **2018**, four walk-on students were offered **scholarships** to play football for the Wolverines.

Michigan quarterback Shea Patterson made 20 pass completions on 30 attempts during a 2018 game at Notre Dame. Patterson was named the Wolverines' Team Offensive Player of the Year for the season.

Being a college student athlete is hard work. Student athletes have to perform well on the football field and in the classroom. Michigan student athletes must maintain a 2.3 grade point average during their first year. At Michigan, Coach Harbaugh believes his players should major in what he calls a "legitimate major." This means they will be prepared for life after college and after football. This is part of the University of Michigan's commitment to their players' overall well-being.

Many student athletes are given athletic scholarships. An athletic scholarship is a financial aid agreement between the athlete and their college or university. Athletes who do not receive an athletic scholarship can also be "walk-on" members of the team. This means they are on the team, but without athletic financial aid. Michigan typically awards the maximum number of football scholarships allowed, which is 85.

Defensive back Ambry Thomas scored his only career touchdown on a 99-yard kick return versus Notre Dame in 2018.

# Bowl Games

The Wolverines have won the **Hall of Fame Bowl** both times they have played in it.

The Wolverines were favored to win the 2018 Chick-fil-A Peach Bowl. They had won their previous four games against the University of Florida Gators.

After the college football season ends, a rare sports tradition begins. The National Collegiate Athletic Association (NCAA) does not sponsor a **postseason** for the sport of football. Instead, a variety of games called bowl games are played. There are currently 40 bowl games played between college football teams. These games give teams the chance to play rivals or new teams. It is also a chance to compete for respect and wins even after they have finished with the regular season.

The Rose Bowl was among the first bowl games in college football history. Since making their first appearance in 1902, the Wolverines have returned to the Rose Bowl for a total of 20 appearances. They have won the Rose Bowl eight times. Most recently, Michigan competed in the Peach Bowl, where the Florida Gators defeated the Wolverines 41–15.

The 2018 Outback Bowl was the 46th bowl appearance for Michigan. The Wolverines have played in the Outback Bowl four times since 1997.

# The Coaches

**Six** coaches for the Michigan Wolverines are in the **College Football Hall of Fame.**

Jim Harbaugh left a National Football League (NFL) coaching job with the San Francisco 49ers, where he won the National Football Conference Championship and was named the 2011 NFL Coach of the Year, to become Michigan State's head coach.

The first official coaches of the Wolverines were Mike Murphy and Frank Crawford, who held co-positions for the 1891 season. There have been 20 coaches who have claimed the title of Wolverines head coach. Many are remembered for their contributions both to Michigan and to college football.

**FIELDING H. YOST** Among the longest-serving coaches in Michigan history is Fielding H. Yost. He was head coach for 25 seasons, from 1901 to 1923 and 1925 to 1926. His early influence made Michigan the team it is today. Between 1901 and 1905, he turned the Wolverines into a "point-a-minute" team. In 1902, his team scored 644 points and gave up only 12.

**BO SCHEMBECHLER** When Bo Schembechler finished his coaching career that spanned 20 years, from 1969 to 1989, he was a **legend** in Wolverines history. He had 194 wins during his 20 years as head coach. He holds the record for most wins as a Wolverines coach. He also led his team to 13 Big Ten championships. He declined offers to coach elsewhere just to keep coaching the Wolverines.

**JIM HARBAUGH** In 2014, an important member of the Michigan Wolverines family came home. Jim Harbaugh, who played for Michigan from 1983 to 1986, was named head coach on December 30. His first season as coach was 2015. He led his Wolverines to a 10–3 record, and set his sights ahead on continuing to win future seasons.

# The Mascot

Live wolverines Bennie and Biff were a part of Michigan Stadium's dedication ceremonies on October 22, 1927.

Although the University of Michigan has adopted the wolverine as its team's name, there is no costumed mascot that represents the school. No one knows for sure why early Michigan students and alumni were drawn to the wolverine. In 1923, Coach Yost saw a live badger at a University of Wisconsin football game. He was inspired to find a wolverine to join his team on the field.

At first, Yost used a large stuffed wolverine from a fur company. In 1927, 10 live Wolverines were brought to the Detroit Zoo. Yost was able to bring two of these wolverines to Michigan Stadium and carry them in cages to entertain fans. Their names were Bennie and Biff, and they eventually became too **ferocious** to bring to games. Bennie was returned to the Detroit Zoo, but Biff was kept in a habitat on campus.

The Chevrolet Motor Company gave the university another live wolverine in 1937. Students named it Intrepidus, but it never made an appearance on the sideline at a football game. Since then, there has been no named or official mascot for the Wolverines. Alumni and football staff have discussed creating a new mascot for the Wolverines. However, there are no current plans to change this tradition in Michigan.

Wolverines are a type of large weasel. They have not been found in the state of Michigan since the 1860s.

# Legends of the Past

For many players, their time with the Wolverines is the start of a promising football career. These are some of the best-known football players to play for the University of Michigan.

## Tom Brady

Today, Tom Brady is a well-known player in the NFL. However, when he arrived at the University of Michigan to play football, he spent his first two years as a backup quarterback. The lack of playing time was frustrating for Brady. This changed during the 1998 and 1999 seasons, when he started every game. Of the 25 games he started, he led his team to victory 20 times. By the end of his career in Michigan, Brady was among the top players for attempts and completions in the team's history. He is a six-time **Super Bowl** champion with the New England Patriots.

**Position:** Quarterback
**Seasons:** 1996–1999 (Michigan Wolverines), 2000–Present (New England Patriots)
**Born:** August 3, 1977, San Mateo, California

## Vidauntae Charlton

Vidauntae "Taco" Charlton joined the Michigan Wolverines in 2013. He was a strong player from the beginning and played in two games as a freshman. He continued his role as defensive end in 2014, this time taking the field in nine games. In Charlton's junior year, he made 30 tackles and earned a starting position for his senior year. That year, he led his team in sacks, with a total of 10. He was then named to the All-Big Ten defensive first team. Charlton's success in Michigan caught the eye of the Dallas Cowboys. He was **drafted** to the team in the first round of the 2017 NFL draft.

**Position:** Defensive End
**Seasons:** 2013–2016 (Michigan Wolverines), 2017–Present (Dallas Cowboys)
**Born:** November 7, 1994 , Pickerington, Ohio

## Mason Cole

Mason Cole graduated from high school a semester early and enrolled at the University of Michigan in January of 2014. He participated in the team's spring practice, and impressed the Michigan coaches when practice for the 2014 season began that fall. Cole was part of the starting lineup in the Wolverines' first game that season. He was the first freshman offensive lineman in Michigan history to start a season opener. During that game, he helped set a single-game offensive record for the Wolverines when they went 350 yards on 36 carries. In 2016, Cole was named to the All-Big Ten offensive second team. Cole was drafted by the Arizona Cardinals in 2018.

**Position:** Center Offensive Lineman
**Seasons:** 2014–2017 (Michigan Wolverines), 2018–Present (Arizona Cardinals)
**Born:** March 28, 1996, Chicago, Illinois

## Brandon Graham

Brandon Graham joined the Wolverines as a linebacker, but found a better fit as a defensive end. In 2009, Graham was chosen by ESPN as the 10th best player in the Big Ten. Brandon Graham's final football game as a college player was the 2010 Senior Bowl. The bowl is played by the best college players in the country. Graham earned **Most Valuable Player (MVP)** honors in the game, which came as no surprise to the Michigan fans who had watched him since 2006. Graham joined the Philadelphia Eagles in the first round of the 2010 NFL draft and was part of their winning Super Bowl team in 2018.

**Position:** Defensive End
**Seasons:** 2006–2009 (Michigan Wolverines), 2010–Present (Philadelphia Eagles)
**Born:** April 3, 1988, Detroit, Michigan

# All-Time Records

## 389

### Single-Game Passing Yards

John Navarre gained a total of 389 yards in a game against Iowa on October 4, 2003, setting the highest passing record in Wolverines history.

## 64

### Most Field Goals Made

Between 2003 and 2006, Garrett Rivas made 64 field goals, a career high for a Michigan Wolverines player.

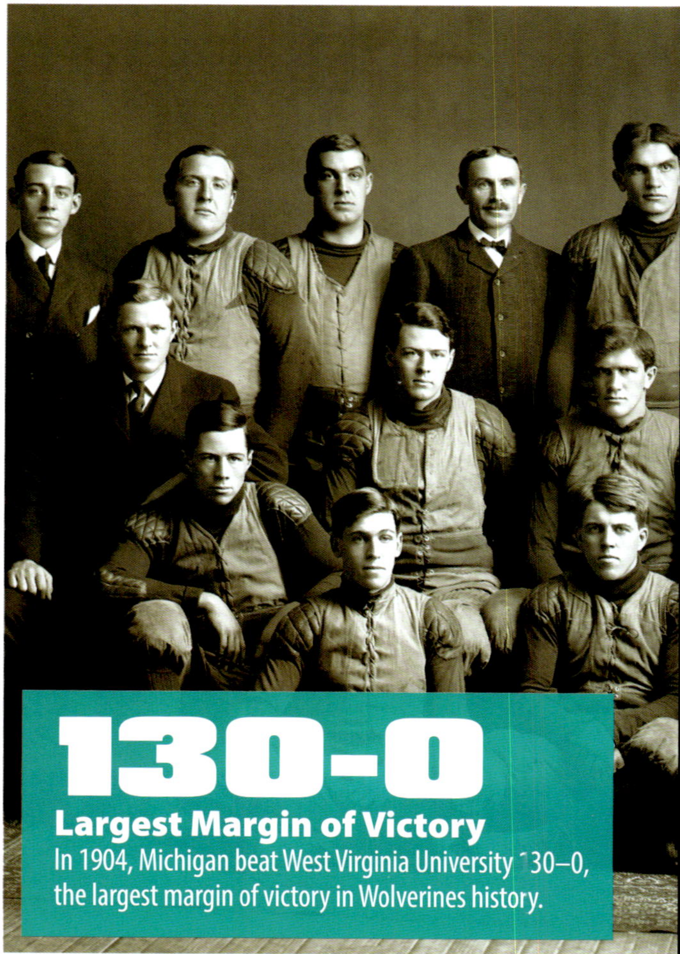

## 130-0

### Largest Margin of Victory

In 1904, Michigan beat West Virginia University 130–0, the largest margin of victory in Wolverines history.

# 388
## Total Draft Picks
As of the 2018 draft, there have been a total of 388 NFL draft picks from Michigan.

# 50
## Longest Winning Streak
Between 1901 and 1907, Michigan won 50 games in a row, the longest winning streak for the Wolverines.

# Timeline

Throughout the team's history, the Michigan Wolverines have had many memorable events that have become defining moments for the team and its fans.

**1969**
The Wolverines beat number-one ranked Ohio State, starting the "Ten-Year War" and deepening the rivalry between the two teams.

Between the years of 1901 to 1904, Michigan does not lose a single game.

1900 1920 1940 1960

**1901**
Fielding Yost takes on his role as the first important coach in Michigan.

**1940**
Tom Harmon wins the first Heisman trophy for the Wolverines.

**1950**
Michigan wins in the Snow Bowl over rival Ohio State Buckeyes.

### The Future

The University of Michigan has one of the greatest football teams in the country. This has been true since nearly the beginning of college football. The Wolverines want to continue to be the best. As they keep up their winning records, the Wolverines draw fans in with their big plays and long rivalries. With Coach Harbaugh leading the way, the Wolverines look to defend their place as the all-time win leader in college football for many years to come.

**1989**
Bo Schembechler retires with 194 wins, ending one of Michigan's most successful eras.

*In 2014, Jim Harbaugh is named head coach.*

1980 2000 2020

**2010**
Michigan Stadium is renovated, reclaiming the title of the biggest college stadium in the country from Penn State's stadium.

**2018**
The Wolverines play in their 47th bowl game, the 2018 Peach Bowl in Atlanta, Georgia.

# Write a Biography

## Life Story

A person's life story can be the subject of a book. This kind of book is called a biography. Biographies often describe the lives of people who have achieved great success. These people may be alive today, or they may have lived many years ago. Reading a biography can help you learn more about a great person.

## Get the Facts

Use this book, and research in the library and on the internet, to find out more about your favorite player. Learn as much about him as you can. What position does he play? What are his statistics in important categories? Has he set any records? Also, be sure to write down key events in the person's life. What was his childhood like? What has he accomplished off the field? Is there anything else that makes this person special or unusual?

## Use the Concept Web

A concept web is a useful research tool. Read the questions in the concept web on the following page. Answer the questions in your notebook. Your answers will help you write a biography.

# Concept Web

## Write a Biography

### Adulthood
- Where does this individual currently reside?
- Does he have a family?

### Your Opinion
- What did you learn from the books you read in your research?
- Would you suggest these books to others?
- Was anything missing from these books?

### Childhood
- Where and when was this person born?
- Describe his parents, siblings, and friends.
- Did he grow up in unusual circumstances?

### Accomplishments off the Field
- What is this person's life's work?
- Has he received awards or recognition for accomplishments?
- How have this person's accomplishments served others?

### Help and Obstacles
- Did this individual have a positive attitude?
- Did he receive help from others?
- Did this person have a mentor?
- Did this person face any hardships?
- If so, how were the hardships overcome?

### Accomplishments on the Field
- What records does this person hold?
- What key games and plays have defined his career?
- What are his stats in categories important to his position?

### Work and Preparation
- What was this person's education?
- What was his work experience?
- How does this person work?
- What is the process he uses?

# Trivia Time

Take this quiz to test your knowledge of the Michigan Wolverines. The answers are printed upside down under each question.

**1** In which conference do the Wolverines compete?

**A.** The Big Ten Conference

**2** When was the first game of Wolverines football played?

**A.** May 30, 1879

**3** What is Michigan Stadium's nickname?

**A.** The Big House

**4** What are the colors of the University of Michigan Wolverines?

**A.** Maize and blue

**5** Where is Michigan Stadium located?

**A.** Ann Arbor, Michigan

**6** When did the Wolverines get their first official coaches?

**A.** In the 1891 season

**7** How many appearances has Michigan made in the Rose Bowl?

**A.** 20 appearances

**8** Who is the Wolverines' current head coach?

**A.** Jim Harbaugh

**9** For how many years did Bo Schembechler coach in Michigan?

**A.** 20

**10** Which team did the Wolverines defeat 130–0 in 1904?

**A.** West Virginia University

# Key Words

**drafted:** chosen to play professionally in the National Football League during an annual event

**exaggeration:** a statement that makes something out to be more extreme than it really is

**ferocious:** extreme, fierce, and violent

**founding:** the creation of a group or institution

**legend:** an extremely well-known or famous person

**Most Valuable Player (MVP):** the player judged to be most valuable to his team's success

**postseason:** a sporting event that takes place after the end of the regular season

**renovated:** improved or expanded an older building

**rivalry:** competition between different groups or individuals toward the same objective or goal

**Super Bowl:** the NFL's annual championship game between the winning team from the National Football Conference and the winning team from the American Football Conference

# Index

# Log on to www.av2books.com

AV² by Weigl brings you media enhanced books that support active learning. Go to www.av2books.com, and enter the special code found on page 2 of this book. You will gain access to enriched and enhanced content that supplements and complements this book. Content includes video, audio, weblinks, quizzes, a slideshow, and activities.

## AV² Online Navigation

**Audio**
Listen to sections of the book read aloud.

**Book Pages**
AV² pages directly correspond to pages in the book.

**Video**
Watch informative video clips.

**Embedded Weblinks**
Gain additional information for research.

**Key Words**
Study vocabulary, and complete a matching word activity.

**Try This!**
Complete activities and hands-on experiments.

**Quizzes**
Test your knowledge.

**Slideshow**
View images and captions, and prepare a presentation.

**AV² was built to bridge the gap between print and digital. We encourage you to tell us what you like and what you want to see in the future.**

**Sign up to be an AV² Ambassador at www.av2books.com/ambassador.**

Due to the dynamic nature of the internet, some of the URLs and activities provided as part of AV² by Weigl may have changed or ceased to exist. AV² by Weigl accepts no responsibility for any such changes. All media enhanced books are regularly monitored to update addresses and sites in a timely manner. Contact AV² by Weigl at 1-866-649-3445 or av2books@weigl.com with any questions, comments, or feedback.